Holmes Jr. High School
Library

T2-AJH-166

D0618339

TITLE I
HOLMES JR HIGH
2001-02

GALAXY OF SUPERSTARS

Ben Affleck	Lauryn Hill
Backstreet Boys	Jennifer Lopez
Brandy	Ricky Martin
Garth Brooks	Ewan McGregor
Mariah Carey	Mike Myers
Matt Damon	'N Sync
Cameron Diaz	LeAnn Rimes
Celine Dion	Adam Sandler
Leonardo DiCaprio	Britney Spears
Tom Hanks	Spice Girls
Hanson	Jonathan Taylor Thomas
Jennifer Love Hewitt	Venus Williams

CHELSEA HOUSE PUBLISHERS

AR.
92
RIM
3/01
$16.00
Gum Drop
#19920

GALAXY OF SUPERSTARS

LeAnn Rimes

Cathy Alter Zymet

Holmes Jr. High School
Library

CHELSEA HOUSE PUBLISHERS
Philadelphia

Produced by
21st Century Publishing and Communications
a division of Tiger & Dragon International, Corp.
New York, New York
http://www.21cpc.com

Editor: Elaine Andrews
Picture Researcher: Hong Xiao
Electronic Composition and Production: Bill Kannar
Design and Art Direction: Irving S. Berman

CHELSEA HOUSE PUBLISHERS

Editor in Chief: Stephen Reginald
Managing Editor: James D. Gallagher
Production Manager: Pamela Loos
Art Director: Sara Davis
Director of Photography: Judy L. Hasday
Senior Production Editor: Lisa Chippendale
Publishing Coordinator: James McAvoy
Cover Illustration: Brian Wible

Front Cover Photo: Ron Wolfson/London Features International, Ltd.
Back Cover Photo: AP/Wide World Photos

© 1999, 2001 by Chelsea House Publishers, a subsidiary of Haights Cross
Communications. All rights reserved. Printed and bound in the United States
of America.

The Chelsea House World Wide Web site address is
http://www.chelseahouse.com

3 5 7 9 8 6 4 2

Library of Congress Cataloging-in-Publication Data

Zymet, Cathy Alter.
   LeAnn Rimes / Cathy Alter Zymet.
      p.   cm. – (Galaxy of superstars)
   Includes bibliographical references and index.
   Summary: A biography of the country music star who gained popularity
And won a Grammy at a remarkably young age.
   ISBN 0-7910-5152-8 (hc)
   1. Rimes, LeAnn—Juvenile literature. 2. Country musicians—
United States—Biography—Juvenile literature. [1. Rimes, LeAnn.
2. Musicians. 3. Women—Biography. 4. Country music.]
I. Title. II. Title: LeAnn Rimes. III. Series.
ML3930.R56Z96 1998
782.421642'092—dc21
   [B]   98-42799
                                                                          CIP
                                                                       AC MN

Contents

1

LIVING THE DREAM

The lights slowly dimmed in Nashville's famed Grand Ole Opry House. The packed audience began to cheer and applaud, eagerly anticipating another great night of performances in Music City. All eyes were center stage, watching veteran Opry member Jeannie Seely make her way to the spotlight. Her clear voice filled every corner of the theater.

"Ladies and gentlemen, let's all put our hands together and welcome a first-timer to the stage. Introducing Miss LeAnn Rimes!"

The Grand Ole Opry is an integral part of the history of country music itself. Far and away the most venerated institution in all of country music, the Grand Ole Opry is not only a cultural treasure but a vital part of America's rich musical tapestry. And now, just two weeks after her 14th birthday, LeAnn Rimes was about to become part of the Opry's musical fabric.

It is the hope and dream of every country performer to be invited to sing at the Grand Ole Opry. For LeAnn, who started off singing her heart out on the little Opry circuit in Texas, this was a dream come true. LeAnn had always hoped she would eventually make it to the Opry's famed

Striding onto the stage to begin a performance, LeAnn radiates the confidence and spirit that enthralls audiences everywhere. Although still very young, she is living her childhood dream of becoming a top country music star.

stage, but she never thought it would happen so soon. The young singer knew it took some musicians many years before they ever got an opportunity to perform at the famed Opry house. But, after hearing her sing just a few months earlier at Fan Fair, Opry's executive producer Bob Whittaker had extended a personal invitation. (Fan Fair is a week-long series of outdoor concerts and autograph sessions held at the Tennessee State Fair.) Her powerful voice and warm rapport with the audience assured Whittaker that LeAnn would be a perfect addition to the Opry roster.

Preparation for the show that Friday night (September 13, 1996) began at dawn, as 40-foot tractor trailers started unloading trunks filled with everything from T-shirts and tour books to sound and light equipment. LeAnn and her band arrived early that afternoon for their sound check. Before every show, a band does a sound check to make sure that its sound is clear enough to be heard from the back rows in the auditorium. At the Grand Ole Opry, this is hardly a big concern. With the Opry's state-of-the-art sound and lighting systems, as well as its outstanding acoustics, LeAnn's voice would be heard from practically across the street!

Yet, even in a multimillion-dollar complex, the dressing rooms are usually less than glamourous. But LeAnn was used to much worse. Playing in other arenas, she had often dressed in the same place where hockey players had taken off their socks the previous night! LeAnn never complained. When she was younger, she used to sit in her dressing room and play with her Barbies until showtime. For

Accompanied by her parents (at right), LeAnn talks to the media outside Nashville's Grand Ole Opry, where she brought down the house in her debut performance at the age of 14.

tonight's performance, instead of dressing her dolls, she chose her own outfit—light-green pants with a short, matching jacket.

When the Grand Ole Opry moved to its new location in 1974, a small piece of wood was taken from its former site and, in a symbolic gesture of continuity, installed center stage in the new Opry house. Some of country music's biggest stars—from Bill Monroe and Grandpa Jones to Garth Brooks and Reba McEntire—have stood on that sacred piece of wood, delighting audiences of thousands.

"It's a big thrill for me to sing on this stage where so many greats have been," admitted

LeAnn's artistry combines a clear, soaring voice with an emotional expressiveness that touches her listeners almost immediately.

LeAnn before the show. "Just the tradition of the Grand Ole Opry is a big thing. You know you've made it when you get to come on the Grand Ole Opry." And now LeAnn was about to take her place among the giants.

LeAnn strode onto the stage with all the confidence of a seasoned professional, and the crowd gave her the welcome she deserved—applauding, whistling, and stomping their feet. Seconds later, listeners sat mesmerized as LeAnn began to sing her first single, "Blue." The song had climbed the charts all summer, and when the full-length album was released in July 1996, it debuted at number one on the *Billboard* country chart and spent a spectacular 19 weeks there.

The crowd loved LeAnn, and all those who had heard "Blue" on the radio that summer became her chorus. Before beginning her next number, she announced to her fans, "It's been a lifelong dream since I was really little to sing on the Opry." Then, holding her wireless microphone lightly between her fingers, LeAnn broke into Patsy Montana's signature song, "I Want To Be a Cowboy's Sweetheart." Montana, who had spent 82 years on the road entertaining audiences of all ages, had died four months earlier. Now LeAnn was paying tribute to her dear friend and mentor. She would go on to write about a similar relationship in her 1997 semi-autobiographical novel, *Holiday in Your Heart.*

For her last song, LeAnn tipped her hat to another great—the Father of Bluegrass and former Opry star Bill Monroe. She performed a rocking version of his classic "Blue Moon of Kentucky," a song that combines the dynamic rhythms of blues and swing music.

Even though she was done with her set, it was not the end of her eventful night. The highlight of LeAnn's evening came when Mike Curb, head of Curb Records, stood by her side and presented his newest star with two plaques. Holding one in each hand, he surprised LeAnn by giving her a gold and a platinum record for her number-one album, *Blue.*

LeAnn felt like she was on top of the world. Off in the wings, her parents, Belinda and Wilbur, were overcome with emotion as they watched their daughter accept her plaques. When it was time for LeAnn to leave the stage, her eyes were glistening with tears.

No matter how many awards she wins, LeAnn never fails to express her delight, and sometimes even surprise, at being honored by the music industry. The young singer is receiving this award for being the most promising new star of country music.

"What a great night!" she exclaimed back-stage after the show.

It was more than that. LeAnn's Opry appearance was a triumph. Her warmth, charm, and amazing voice had won over everyone in the house. Grandparents and grandchildren alike embraced her as though she were one of their own.

LeAnn's widespread appeal has kept her riding high on a wave of success. Being one of the world's hottest new singing sensations is just the beginning for her. With LeAnn's sheer determination to succeed, the future holds limitless possibilities. Ever since she told her parents at the age of five that she was going to sing and become a big star, she has not lost sight of her dream. "If you have a dream or goal," LeAnn advises, "don't stop until you reach it. If you really want to accomplish something, don't let anyone stand in your way. If you truly want to achieve something, then go for it."

This is the story of how LeAnn Rimes did just that. With the support of her family, the love of her fans, and the strength of her own spirit, LeAnn has been able to make all of her wishes come true.

2

A NATURAL

Wilbur and Belinda Rimes were high-school sweethearts who went steady and were married at 17. The newlyweds settled in the small town of Flowood, Mississippi, where Belinda soon found work as a receptionist, and Wilbur sold seismic equipment to oil companies. The young couple quickly fell into the usual routines of working, seeing family and friends, and attending the local Baptist church on Sundays. Even though the couple had full and happy lives, something was still missing. Wilbur and Belinda wanted a child. Eager to start a family, they quickly learned that it would be difficult. Not long after their marriage, doctors told the couple they would not be able to have children. But Belinda still held on to the hope that she would one day be a mother.

For 10 years Wilbur and Belinda tried to have a baby, and for 10 years they had no luck. With each year they spent childless, their vision faded a bit more. Although Belinda saw other women becoming mothers and wondered what was wrong with her, she never lost faith. In 1981, she began praying for a child, and in less than six weeks, Belinda was pregnant. Margaret LeAnn Rimes was

---

LeAnn's natural talent was obvious from an early age. Barely into her teens she performed with the poise and confidence of a seasoned professional.

born on August 28, 1982. Her parents have always called her LeAnn. They also call her their miracle child. Says Belinda, "Wilbur and I agreed that we would devote our lives to her."

Until she was six, LeAnn lived in Flowood, Mississippi—a state that has been home to such musical greats as Muddy Waters, Robert Johnson, and Elvis Presley. LeAnn had an early introduction to music. Both of her parents loved to sing around the house, and people said that Wilbur had perfect pitch. He was also an amateur guitar player. Her parents were thrilled when one day, in front of a living room full of relatives, 18-month-old LeAnn sat in her baby seat and belted out "Jesus Loves Me."

LeAnn soon took her show on the road, singing to her parents from her car seat. "It's something every mother would probably love to see her little girl do," recalls Belinda. "I've seen her when she was a little girl wake up in the backseat, get up and sing, and lie right back down and go to sleep."

LeAnn recollects similar memories in her novel, *Holiday in Your Heart*: "My favorite memories about Dad and our music come from singing in the car. We sang everywhere he drove, whether we were on our way to a show or the grocery store. Dad drove old cars that always had a hump on the floor of the backseat. I asked what was under the hump and he told me the 'singing monster.' He said the monster ate little girls who sang off key."

Belinda and Wilbur encouraged their daughter's talents. They had a large record collection, and LeAnn loved to sit and listen to country singers like Reba McEntire, Wynonna,

Belinda and Wilbur Rimes stand proudly beside their daughter. Knowing LeAnn was special and confident she would succeed, Belinda and Wilbur made tremendous sacrifices in encouraging her talent and guiding her career.

and Patsy Cline. But even then, LeAnn's tastes included other kinds of music. She also listened to Barbra Streisand and Judy Garland. No matter who she listened to, LeAnn could recreate every song she heard. Looking back, her mother says LeAnn's desire to sing was so strong, it was "like she knew what she came into this world wanting to do."

Wilbur recognized LeAnn's natural talent and began making tapes of her perfectly pitched voice. Every weekend, Wilbur sat his daughter next to his tape recorder, and LeAnn sang along as her father played guitar. These first "studio sessions" produced tapes of LeAnn singing "You Are My Sunshine," "Getting To Know You," and "Have Mercy" by the Judds. One afternoon, LeAnn surprised her dad and taught him how to yodel. She just listened once to "All Around the Water Tank" and showed him the proper way to do it. It would not be long before yodeling became LeAnn's trademark.

Besides singing, LeAnn loved to tap-dance. A true performer, she began taking lessons at the age of two and, at age four, dressed in red gingham, she tap-danced in her first show. Her dance teacher noticed her natural charm and bubbly personality and suggested that Wilbur and Belinda enter her in some local talent contests.

Her parents weren't sure if LeAnn was old enough to handle the pressure of competing. But LeAnn told them that she wanted a chance to win. To her, the opportunity to perform was just as important as winning. That was when Belinda and Wilbur promised that they would do everything they could to get LeAnn started.

LeAnn entered her first talent contest when she was only six. For weeks, she diligently practiced "Getting To Know You," rehearsing over and over until she got it just right. When her parents drove her to the show, she was more than ready to perform— she was ready to win.

Wilbur thought differently. When he found out that the other children competing were twice as old as LeAnn, he lost all hope of her winning. And even though LeAnn performed her song to perfection, he did not believe that the judges would vote for her. Too nervous to wait for the contest results, he left Belinda and LeAnn at the show and spent the rest of the day hunting raccoons in the Mississippi woods.

Wilbur arrived home just in time to see LeAnn carrying a huge, first-place trophy through the front door. She had done so well, in fact, that she took home five awards! At that moment, Wilbur knew he would never doubt his daughter's talents or abilities again. He told LeAnn, "If this is what you want to do, I'll never miss another contest. We'll go for it."

LeAnn's win that day changed her life forever. She told her parents that she was going to grow up to be a big star. That day would come sooner than anyone ever imagined. Shortly after the talent show, Wilbur began making phone calls and setting up auditions for his daughter. Unfortunately, not a lot was going on in Mississippi. If LeAnn was going to break into show business, the Rimeses would have to look elsewhere.

In search of better opportunities for LeAnn, Wilbur requested a job transfer to Dallas, Texas. After selling his truck and hunting dogs to make some extra money, the family headed off to their new life. The Rimeses had no way of knowing what lay down the road, but Wilbur and Belinda did know that whether it be heartache or happiness, LeAnn was much too talented not to be given a chance. Little did they know that within months, LeAnn would surpass everyone's expectations—including her own.

3

HEART OF TEXAS

Once in Texas, Wilbur thought the opportunities for LeAnn were as big as the Lone Star State. The family moved into a two-bedroom apartment in Garland, just 15 miles from the bright lights of Dallas. In their living room, a multitrack recorder and a sound-mixing board competed for space among the couches and television. Instead of watching her favorite shows, LeAnn worked with her father on picking out song material, arranging the songs to best feature her voice, rehearsing for performances, and recording her music.

Fully settled into her new life, LeAnn was anxious to start auditioning for local concerts. Her favorite song to sing for auditions was Patsy Cline's "Crazy." Because she was so young, Wilbur had to explain to LeAnn that the song was a heartbreaking story about someone losing her love.

LeAnn's career took off, and before long she was getting steady work at local showcases. Her first big break came when she auditioned for a regular spot on the Dallas–Fort Worth Metroplex Oprys. This is a circuit of "little Opry" stages operating in Garland, Mesquite, Greenville, and Grapevine. Texas Metroplex shows usually take place on

In Dallas, the entertainment and cultural heart of Texas, LeAnn launched her career with appearances in local country music shows.

weekends, and every Saturday night, Wilbur and Belinda drove LeAnn from one show to another, making the rounds and adding more and more fans along the way.

Her schedule may have been demanding, but LeAnn never complained. She was too determined to prove her talents. Remembers Belinda, "She'd be sleeping in the car as we drove to the next Opry, and then she'd get up on the stage and sing 'Crazy' and then get right back in the car and go to sleep."

LeAnn showed so much talent that her parents took her to New York City when she was six to compete against girls twice her age for the lead role in the Broadway show *Annie II*. Though she was one of the 11 kids who made it to the finals, the other girls were older and had more experience working in the theater. The casting director told her that even though she was wonderful, they thought she was too young to carry the show.

Although one of LeAnn's earliest rejections, she thought it was an important experience. To help her get over her disappointment, her parents bought her a dog. LeAnn named it Sandy—the name of Annie's dog.

A year later, LeAnn made her acting debut, delighting Dallas audiences as Tiny Tim in a musical production of Charles Dickens's *A Christmas Carol*. LeAnn's glowing stage presence really came through, and she received rave reviews in all the local newspapers. Still, at seven years old, LeAnn realized that she wanted to have more than just a career on the stage. She wanted to sing more than anything. It seemed that LeAnn could not think of anything other than music, and her mother began to worry that her daughter was missing out on a regular childhood. Because LeAnn was always on the road performing, she had no friends her own age.

That all changed when LeAnn started school. She entered Club Hill Elementary School as a second grader and was so outgoing that she easily made friends. But her best friend was always music, and she promised her parents that she would keep up her straight-A average if she could still continue to sing on weekends.

Around this time LeAnn met the man who would become the most influential person in her early career—Johnnie High. She auditioned in Fort Worth for a slot in Johnnie High's Country Music Revue, the long-running weekend show that has launched the careers of countless country singing stars such as Gary Morris and Linda Davis. When LeAnn sang her rendition of "Crazy" for Johnnie, he reacted very strongly—he got goose bumps! High signed her on the spot. After seeing so much talent pass through his door over the years, he knew that LeAnn was something special.

LeAnn quickly became a favorite on Johnnie High's weekly show, and it was not long before she found herself in the best slot on the program— going on last. She closed every show to a standing ovation. Dressed in frilly white dresses, LeAnn sang classic country and western tunes. Backed by a band of local Dallas musicians, with her father playing guitar, LeAnn built up a following. Every week, people came from all over just to hear her sing. In the course of six

LeAnn's warm and friendly smile and outgoing personality delighted Dallas audiences. The young performer quickly became a favorite with country music fans.

years, LeAnn performed over 300 consecutive Saturday nights, always to a full house. Every time she appeared onstage, says Johnnie, "She never forgot a word or messed up once. She was perfection onstage."

But LeAnn had still another stage to conquer. In 1990, at eight years old, she made her first appearance on *Star Search*, a televised talent show hosted by Ed McMahon. Each week, actors, models, dancers, comedians, and singers performed for a panel of judges. The winners returned the following week to face new challengers in their categories.

LeAnn decided to sing a Marty Robbins song, "Don't Worry About Me," in the Best Female Vocalist category. Onstage, she was not a bit nervous, even in front of the cameras, and the audience and judges loved her. LeAnn won her round and became a two-week champion. After performing for a television audience of millions, LeAnn was even more convinced that she wanted a career in show business.

A self-described workaholic, LeAnn continued to perform every Saturday night in Johnnie High's show. She also began singing the national anthem a cappella at Dallas home games, wowing audiences at Sidekicks, Texas Rangers, and Mavericks events. When she was 10, she sang "The Star-Spangled Banner" for the Dallas Cowboys at Texas Stadium. Asked what it felt like to perform in front of thousands of people, LeAnn recalls, "That was exciting. I wasn't even nervous—I kind of got over that at a young age."

At one of these home events, a Fort Worth disc jockey and composer heard LeAnn's incredible singing and remarked, "The hair stood up on my arm. I forgot all about her age. You just don't hear anybody sing 'The Star-Spangled Banner' that good." The man who witnessed LeAnn's performance that day was Bill Mack. He would be the next to play an important role in LeAnn's rise to stardom.

4

OUT OF THE BLUE

Bill Mack has been in the country music business for more than 42 years. As both a disc jockey and a composer, he has worked with famed stars such as Elvis Presley and Jerry Lee Lewis and has had his songs recorded by country fixtures including Bill Monroe and Conway Twitty.

In 1959, a young Bill Mack, strumming his guitar, composed a ballad he called "Blue." Consisting of only five chords, the song took him just 15 minutes to write. Bill decided to give "Blue" to his idol at the time, Patsy Cline, feeling as if it was really *her* song. Bill recorded a demo and, keeping his fingers crossed, sent it off to Patsy's label. The tape made it into the hands of Patsy's husband, Charlie Dick, who thought it would be perfect for his wife. But Patsy never got the chance to record "Blue." She died in a tragic plane crash in 1963.

Bill Mack could not imagine anyone else but Patsy singing his song. He put the song away in a drawer and did not pull it out again until he heard LeAnn Rimes sing "The Star-Spangled Banner." Bill knew right then and there that she was the one who had to sing his "Blue."

Meanwhile, Wilbur Rimes was in the middle of choosing

LeAnn interprets a song with her incredible voice and honest emotions that come straight from her heart. The first time she heard the song "Blue," she knew right away it was perfect for her.

songs for LeAnn's first album. He planned to produce her record on an independent label and needed material that would really show off his daughter's distinctive voice. When Wilbur received a package from Bill Mack, he immediately sat down and played "Blue." Unfortunately, Wilbur thought the song sounded "too old" for LeAnn. Recalls LeAnn, "My dad didn't like that song when he first got it. I asked him for it, but he wouldn't give it to me and he threw it away. But I finally found it and played it, and I loved it."

LeAnn knew the song was just right for her, but she still had to convince her father. After listening to the song a few times, she added a little yodel to "Blue." When she sang her version for Wilbur, he was entranced. "That's when I fell in love with it," he says. "LeAnn put that little yodel lick in it and she really transformed it. She made it her own." Wilbur added "Blue" to LeAnn's song list and then told Bill Mack they wanted to record his song.

Although LeAnn was riding high, with plans for her first album being finalized, her life back home in Garland was not going as well. School was becoming an increasingly unhappy place for LeAnn. She was having trouble balancing school with performing, and her classmates were finding it difficult to deal with LeAnn's rising fame. The young star could not understand her fellow students' jealous behavior. She could not see why her friends thought she was so different, especially since she considered herself to be a normal kid—one who just happened to have a talent for singing. On her last day of sixth grade, LeAnn discovered that someone had

smashed eggs on her locker. She asked her parents if she could leave school and study with a private tutor. They agreed.

With LeAnn home more, Wilbur decided to quit his job to manage her career full-time. He soon met Lyle Walker, an attorney who was also co-owner of the famous Norman Petty studio in Clovis, New Mexico—the same studio at which Buddy Holly and Roy Orbison

Famed country singer Patsy Cline never got to sing "Blue," the song written especially for her. When LeAnn heard the song, she made it her own, and "Blue" launched the young singer into her phenomenal rise to stardom.

had recorded some of their greatest hits. Walker was looking for new talent to record, and he talked LeAnn and Wilbur into coming to Clovis to make an album. At the time, no one had any idea that the album LeAnn was about to record would be the spark that ignited her career.

LeAnn had never been in a recording studio before. She stood under a hanging microphone and faced her father, who watched from behind the thick glass of the control booth. Next to him sat various technicians. Seeing all of this for the first time made LeAnn nervous. But once the music sounded in her headphones and she started to sing the first few notes of "Blue," LeAnn began to relax and have some fun. She did most of the songs in one take—including "Blue," the song that would change her life.

In 1994, *All That* was released on the Nor Va Jak independent label. The cover of the album showed LeAnn dressed in a white-fringed Western suit. First available only at LeAnn's shows and at stores in the Dallas area, *All That* sold so well, an estimated 15,000 copies in a year, that word filtered back to Nashville.

Soon, LeAnn was auditioning for Jimmy Bowen, then head of Capitol Records in Nashville. When he heard LeAnn sing, he saw enormous potential but thought that she was too young to embark on a recording career. "He told me to come back when I was eighteen because he didn't want to take on a child," remembers LeAnn. "He thought I wasn't really old enough to handle it. He was right to tell me to wait, but I couldn't. I really wanted it."

Even though Bowen decided not to handle LeAnn, others were jumping at the chance to sign her. EMI, Decca, and MCA/Nashville all wanted to add LeAnn to their rosters. Wilbur, however, was never satisfied with any of the offers. He decided to hold out until the right deal came along.

In the spring of 1995, Mike Curb, the owner and chairman of Curb Records, listened to *All That*. "Someone sent me her CD," he begins. "I was leaving town with my family to drive up to the Smoky Mountains. I have two daughters about LeAnn's age. When I put her CD on, everyone just turned their heads and said, 'Who is that?' We played it all the way up and all the way back, over and over. On the way home, I stopped at a pay phone and called her management and said, 'We are interested in this artist very much.'"

Mike Curb, a former lieutenant governor of California, had shaped the careers of teen acts like the Osmonds and Shaun Cassidy and was now a major player in the music industry. In fact, Curb made a business out of finding young singers and catapulting them into superstardom. He wanted to add LeAnn to his book of success stories since he was certain she would be the next big thing in country music. Looking to sign her immediately, Curb made Wilbur the kind of deal that was impossible to refuse: Mike Curb promised Wilbur that he could still manage LeAnn's career. Curb also committed to signing LeAnn to a multi-album deal.

LeAnn accepts one of her many awards with her father behind her. Concerned because LeAnn was so young and success was putting her on the fast track, Wilbur became her full-time manager so he could better guide her career.

The Rimeses were convinced that Curb was the right label for LeAnn. She would be nurtured by a company that was interested in seeing her grow as a performer. At the same time, because the family was still involved in her management, Wilbur and Belinda would remain equally involved in LeAnn's career.

In May 1995, after two months of negotiations, LeAnn signed her contract with Curb Records. An announcement was sent out which included a statement from Dennis Hannon, Curb vice president and general manager. "We are thrilled with her incredible talent and anxious to introduce her to country radio. Nineteen ninety-six will be a very exciting year for us all." LeAnn was just 13 years old and about to enter the most exhilarating phase of her young life.

5

RECIPE FOR SUCCESS

Mike Curb gave LeAnn one year to make her album. This relaxed deadline more than pleased her. It meant that she could take all the time she needed to work on her music, select her songs, and get everything just right before she ever stepped foot in the recording studio.

LeAnn decided to go with two songs that appeared on her independent release *All That.* Now two years older, she rerecorded the ballad "I'll Get Even with You," as well as her signature song, "Blue." With her 13-year-old voice, LeAnn gave the songs a new sense of maturity. Choosing the rest of the material for the album presented more of a challenge. LeAnn had a strong say in the kind of music she wanted to record, but at the same time, Curb wanted the new album to distinguish itself against others on the market. They decided to do something a little different: LeAnn would record a combination of old and new country sounds.

Songs like "Blue," "Honestly," and "Fade to Blue," are more traditional in style, while "One Way Ticket (Because I Can)" and "Good Lookin' Man" lean toward a

---

LeAnn's singing, described as "warm" and "throaty," has been compared to that of Patsy Cline. But her incredible success also includes the ability to choose the right songs to show off both her voice and her talent as a natural performer.

Holmes Jr. High School Library

more up-tempo and current sound. LeAnn also chose to record two pieces by one of her favorite songwriters, Deborah Allen—"Hurt Me" and "My Baby."

It was Mike Curb who decided to have LeAnn sing the classic song "Cattle Call," a ballad that had been a number-one hit for Eddy Arnold in 1955. Mike hoped he could coax Eddy out of retirement to sing a duet with LeAnn. After hearing a tape of LeAnn singing, it did not take much persuasion to get Eddy back into the studio to rerecord his famous song with LeAnn. He thought that LeAnn had one of the best voices he had ever heard. LeAnn felt the same way about him. In the liner notes of her album she wrote a personal note to Eddy: "What an honor to sing with such a great man and a living legend."

LeAnn was so immersed in making music that she began trying her hand at song writing herself. With the help of composers Ron Grimes and Jon Rutherford, she wrote "Talk to Me," which she recorded for the Curb debut album.

All in all, LeAnn recorded the tracks for her album in four different studios. When the album was in its final stages, Curb began to send out press releases announcing the solo effort of the company's newest star. Curb wanted the media to be well aware of LeAnn Rimes and set about making a stir. In April 1996, rather than releasing the full album, Curb Records began to circulate a four-song sampler and electronic press kit to radio stations. The sampler included "The Light in Your Eyes," "Hurt Me," "My Baby," and of course, "Blue." Originally "The Light in Your Eyes" was slated to be the first single off the album, but Curb instead decided to release "Blue" when it became apparent that radio stations—and listeners—loved it.

Included in the press kit was the story of how "Blue" came to be, and every time the disc jockeys played the song, they told the same story to their listeners. The stations began playing "Blue" several times a day, with more and more people calling up daily to request the song.

At first the radio stations were not prepared for the kind of reaction they received from their listeners. Remembers Kevin O'Neal, a disc jockey from Philadelphia's WXTU, "We put it on the air one time and instantly got calls from record stores from people walking in specifically wanting to buy that song. Originally we were concerned about playing a record that sounds too much like yesterday, but with LeAnn's youth and freshness this record comes home. I can't think of anybody else who could have sung this song and made it work."

As soon as Mac Daniels, a program director from Washington, D.C.'s WMZQ, began playing "Blue," his station was bombarded with requests from fans. On an evening when he gave the song to night deejay Scott Carpenter, the response was so overwhelming, Carpenter had to play it three times. He was getting calls from kids, from their grandparents, and from everyone in between—all asking to hear that new song from LeAnn Rimes.

Neil McGinely, operations director for

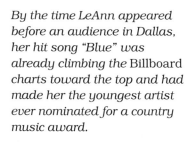

By the time LeAnn appeared before an audience in Dallas, her hit song "Blue" was already climbing the Billboard *charts toward the top and had made her the youngest artist ever nominated for a country music award.*

Atlanta's WKHX-FM and WYAY-FM remarks, "Our phones have absolutely blown off the hook. It's our number one most-requested song." And the list goes on. The last time a song created such a stir was when Billy Ray Cyrus's "Achy Breaky Heart" hit the airwaves.

In May 1996, "Blue" debuted at 49 on *Billboard*'s country chart. Five weeks later, it was number 12. And for two weeks straight, the song remained at number 10. For LeAnn to have this kind of success, without a video on television or a record in stores, was just plain remarkable. To show her appreciation LeAnn spent an entire day calling radio stations and thanking them for their support.

On June 4, when the single was finally released to retail stores, fans bought more than 100,000 copies. In less than one week, "Blue" became the number-one-selling single, and it retained that position for 20 consecutive weeks.

"Blue" was so popular that Curb decided to put together a video for Country Music Television (CMT) and the Nashville Network (TNN). Music videos act as extra promotion for an artist's album. The only drawback is that these three- or four-minute music clips are not cheap to make. The video version of "Blue" may have helped to sell the single, but it cost Curb Records thousands of dollars to produce. In the highly competitive world of music, the price of video taping an artist's song has skyrocketed. Today the money being spent is between $30,000 and $200,000, with the average cost at about $75,000. Curb believed that the expense was worth it and put out the word early that the video of "Blue" was about to be released.

After LeAnn's incredible success with "Blue," music channels could not wait to air the video version of the most talked-about song of the year. The video was filmed in Austin, Texas, at the location of a natural spring-fed pool, Barton Springs. LeAnn is taped in different shots. First she is singing "Blue" in a studio. Then she is lounging poolside, wearing movie-star sunglasses and flirting with boys.

As the summer progressed, LeAnn put the finishing touches on her full-length album. At the same time, Curb Records was deciding what sort of picture of LeAnn they should use

Minus one of her dazzling and sometimes controversial stage outfits, LeAnn poses with a fan at her own autograph booth during Nashville's annual Fan Fair.

on its cover. LeAnn wanted a photo that showed her youthful energy. On the other side of the spectrum, Curb wanted to go with a more mature look. Even though LeAnn was a teenager, she and Curb did not want to alienate their older record buyers. In an attempt to attract *all* record buyers, Curb went with a slightly alluring picture of LeAnn wearing a long dress with a lace top. Curb's desire to show LeAnn looking older than her years would soon come back to haunt the young singer.

On June 11, 1996, just weeks before the release of LeAnn's debut album, she performed at Fan Fair. The yearly event gives fans a chance to meet their favorite country music musicians and offers curious industry executives a chance to check out new talent.

Wearing a long, flowing black dress, LeAnn took to the stage under damp skies and began singing the first lines of "Blue." Looking out at the crowd, she noticed members of the audience singing along, note for note. LeAnn was amazed. After the show, she told her mother that she could not believe so many people knew her song. On the strength of just one song, LeAnn had won legions of fans, and they could not wait until her album hit the shelves. The album was originally scheduled to be released in September, but demand was so great that Curb Records decided to move the date up to July.

In the days leading up to the release of her debut album, LeAnn made a round of appearances, giving interviews and drumming up a lot of excitement. Curb Records wanted to make sure that everyone with a stereo knew all about LeAnn's new album. Mike Curb was counting on selling LeAnn to a whole world of music lovers.

6

BEYOND THE DREAM

On July 9, 1996, LeAnn's first major-label album, *Blue*, went on sale and was an immediate success. It debuted at number one on the *Billboard* country chart and stayed there a spectacular 19 weeks, more than any other album during the year. Such a feat made LeAnn the youngest singer in history to have a debut album go straight to the top in the first weeks of release.

Blue also hit number three on the pop *Billboard* 200 album chart, cementing LeAnn's crossover status by selling as many copies as albums by such stars as Metallica and Celine Dion. It went gold in England, double platinum in Canada, and triple platinum in Australia, where LeAnn was proclaimed that country's best-selling female country music artist of all time. When LeAnn celebrated her 14th birthday on August 28, 1996, her album had already gone gold. By the time she sang at the Grand Ole Opry in September, she had added a platinum record to her collection.

Besides being a commercial success, *Blue* was a critical success as well. The album was widely applauded in nationwide reviews. Said *Newsday*: "Nothing kidlike about

Grand Ole Opry's host Vince Gill presents Newcomer of the Year nominee LeAnn following her debut performance. Her "first" at the famed music shrine brought her success beyond her childhood dreams.

it. Rimes' is a voice that is mature and highly nuanced. LeAnn rises to greatness. *Blue* is a classic." The *Dallas Morning News* reported, "Teenage country crooner sounds like an old hand."

But the fact remained that LeAnn was not the "old hand" the critics praised. She was just a teenager. When fans started reading articles about LeAnn, they found it hard to believe she was only 13. To convince the public that she was not lying about her age, LeAnn and her parents appeared on *Entertainment Tonight*. In front of millions, LeAnn proudly showed her birth certificate.

Aside from looking too much like an adult, LeAnn was criticized for singing songs with adult lyrics. She has answered her critics in interviews, explaining, "I'm really not that conscious of the maturity of the lyrics. I'm trying to appeal to all ages, and I try to do great songs. I don't sing about drinking and smoking and going into a bar and that kind of stuff, because that's not me. But I don't think I have to experience a lyric to sing it, and I'm not saying I did experience all the lyrics I sing."

LeAnn was suddenly getting more attention than she had ever imagined. Her whirlwind of success continued throughout the summer of 1996, culminating on August 13, the day the Country Music Association (CMA) announced the nominations for its 1996 awards. In country music, winning a CMA award is the equivalent of an actor's getting an Oscar or an Emmy.

The nominees were announced on the steps of the Grand Ole Opry house and LeAnn heard

Nationwide critical success shined the spotlight on LeAnn, who constantly had to prove she was still just a teenager. Her celebrity status put her in the company of New York City's mayor, Rudolph Giuliani, and singer Roberta Flack.

her name called twice: "Blue" was in the running for Single of the Year, and she was also nominated for the Horizon Award, an honor presented to the newcomer who had made the most progress during the previous year. Whether she won or not, LeAnn was the youngest person in CMA's history to ever be nominated. Until then, Tanya Tucker had held that honor, having been nominated when she was just 14.

LeAnn had won many ribbons and trophies in her life, but for her to be nominated for two CMAs was victory enough. In an interview with *TV Guide* she said, "This has been the biggest surprise in my life. I really didn't expect it, because this is my first year in the business.

LeAnn's rise to fame included performing in Nashville with Randy Travis (left) and George Jones. She not only performed with these country music veterans, she also co-hosted the show.

I'm not really expecting an award, but just to be nominated is really neat for me. To think that the people in the business think so highly of me and my music is really an honor. I'll be at the show with bells on."

LeAnn wasn't actually wearing bells when she appeared at the 1996 Country Music Association Awards that October, but she still managed to create a stir. Invited to participate in two segments that evening, LeAnn opened the show by singing "Blue," wearing—what else?—a blue velvet top and matching full-length taffeta skirt. Before she took the stage, host Vince Gill told an audience filled with some of the most famous stars in country that

LeAnn would be the next big star of country music. When LeAnn finished singing, the crowd gave her a huge standing ovation. Vince Gill invited her back up on the stage to take another bow. Then he joked that she was so good, she ought to host the show!

For her second appearance that night, LeAnn changed into a blue pantsuit and sang Patsy Montana's "I Want To Be a Cowboy's Sweetheart." Next, holding up a plaque, she and Marty Stuart inducted Patsy into the Country Music Hall of Fame. LeAnn did not win any awards that evening, but that did not dampen her spirits. She had already won the respect of all the hottest names in country—such as George Strait and Garth Brooks—who had heard her sing that night. LeAnn also won some brand new fans. A week after the CMA presentation, sales of *Blue* doubled.

LeAnn had succeeded in grabbing the attention of the nation. Suddenly, articles about her rise to fame started to appear in more and more magazines and newspapers. Most stories compared LeAnn to teen sensations of the past. Both Tanya Tucker and Brenda Lee had number-one songs when they were only 14. That, however, is where the similarities end. LeAnn is definitely of her own time, the star of a new generation of hitmakers.

By the end of 1996, LeAnn's records were selling faster than Curb could press them. The week of December 16, her third single off of *Blue*, "One Way Ticket (Because I Can)," hit number one on the *Radio & Records*

Her star showed no signs of declining as LeAnn appeared with Santa at the White House Christmas Tree lighting ceremony in 1996. Audiences also saw her nationwide on the Oprah Winfrey show about "People Who Made It in 1996," where she sang "Blue" to a standing ovation.

chart, making her the youngest country singer in history to have a number-one song. What's more, when "One Way Ticket" hit the top, LeAnn became the first young female recording artist with both a number-one song and a number-one album on the charts at the same time.

She was also attracting some fairly unusual fans. When *Rolling Stone* magazine asked Kiss rocker Gene Simmons to name his top-ten favorite albums of the year, LeAnn's was top on his list. President Bill Clinton was also a big admirer. He and First Lady Hillary Rodham Clinton invited LeAnn to the White House to help light the famous White House Christmas Tree. "The president was real nice," LeAnn remembers. "He told me that he had my CD and he enjoyed my music—he's a big fan of mine."

That Christmas season, LeAnn mingled with all sorts of celebrities. She chatted with Jay Leno on his *Tonight Show*, sang to Oprah Winfrey on her show, and as spokesperson for Target Stores, made a commercial with Bugs Bunny, Tweety Bird, and all the other Looney Tunes characters.

As the year came to a close, LeAnn's life in the spotlight was only just beginning. The New Year held endless possibilities for the young singer, as well as a few surprises. Nineteen ninety-seven would bring more success than LeAnn had ever imagined.

7

ON TOP OF THE WORLD

For LeAnn, 1997 began as 1996 had ended—on a high note. On January 27, she picked up an American Music Award (AMA) for Favorite New Country Artist. Accepting her award, LeAnn admitted to everyone seated in Los Angeles's Shrine Auditorium, "Everything that has happened to me in the last six months usually happens to an artist in two or three years. Getting this award to go along with everything else is overwhelming."

LeAnn's popularity showed no signs of flagging. She was in such demand that Curb Records decided to keep the momentum rolling by releasing another album. On February 11, the company released *Unchained Melody/The Early Years*, which contained mostly songs off of LeAnn's earlier *All That*. Her thrilled fans rushed out to buy LeAnn's newest record. The album became an instant smash and debuted as the number-one album in America. And, going for the hat trick, LeAnn scored two Grammys. She won for Best Female Country Vocal for "Blue" and for Best New Artist. "I'm going to go out to dinner tonight," she told the audience after winning her second award. "At my age I don't know how else I can celebrate."

Being on top of the country music world in 1997 seems to make it easy for LeAnn to juggle three Academy of Country Music awards at once: Song of the Year, Single Record of the Year, and Top New Female Vocalist.

But LeAnn did not sit back and rest on her laurels. As a follow-up to *Unchained Melody/ The Early Years*, she recorded and released her third album, *You Light Up My Life: Inspirational Songs*. This deeply spiritual album contains standards such as "Amazing Grace" and "God Bless America," along with newer material such as "How Do I Live." This album went triple platinum and contributed to making LeAnn the top recording artist of 1997.

With more musical accomplishments to her credit than most people see in a lifetime— awards from every major music organization, multiplatinum albums that continue to chart as best-sellers—LeAnn was ready to tackle other areas of the entertainment arena. With the help of veteran Nashville author Tom Carter, LeAnn wrote a beautiful book called *Holiday in Your Heart*. The story is a simple but universal one. It tells the tale of Anna Lee (could it be LeAnn?), a teenage country-singing phenomenon who is ready to make her name in Nashville and across the nation. The only thing that threatens her happiness is her beloved Grandma Teeden, who has been stricken with an illness and has remained in the family's native Mississippi. Although her grandpa urges her to come home, Anna decides to stay in Nashville to get her career in gear.

Of course, Anna Lee's feelings about love and loyalty are turned around when she meets the mysterious woman known simply as "The Legend," who was an Opry star in her own right years before. The Legend leads Anna Lee on a long journey, during which she discovers that only God and family can keep a holiday in your heart all year 'round.

Loosely autobiographical, LeAnn's own grandmother had died right before LeAnn signed her record deal with Curb. Her first album, *Blue*, is dedicated to her beloved grandmother: "I dedicate this album to my Grandfather, Thad Butler, along with a very special dedication to my Grandmother, Annie Jewell Butler, who passed away in 1994. I love you, Maw Maw!"

In December 1997, *Holiday in Your Heart* was turned into a made-for-TV movie—starring LeAnn and Bernadette Peters. LeAnn showed some impeccable comic timing, and when she and Peters appeared in scenes together, their chemistry was dynamic.

LeAnn had been bit by the acting bug. Her subsequent stint in front of the camera was when she guested on NBC's daytime soap opera *Days of Our Lives*, a show she had watched since the age of two! In the story line, LeAnn plays Madison, a runaway teen. In one scene, she fantasizes that she is having a romance with Eric (Jensen Ackles, and LeAnn's real-life friend), and the two share her first on-screen kiss. According to LeAnn, she had a hard time trying not to laugh.

LeAnn, who taped more than 35 pages of dialogue over two days, remembers, "One of my favorite acting moments came at the beginning when Eric stops Madison after she is caught stealing. I got to be a real pain in the butt. It was fun to be rude because I'm not like that in real life."

The camera clearly loves LeAnn. She comes across as charming and sincere and is a natural

LeAnn's whirlwind schedule includes promoting her semi-autobiographical novel, Holiday in Your Heart, *at a Barnes & Noble bookstore in New York City. She got the acting bug as well when she appeared in a TV dramatization of her book.*

spokesperson. Aside from her commercials for Target Stores, LeAnn is now the voice and face of Samsung. Her telephone commercial features LeAnn chatting a mile a minute on the phone. As she enjoys her gab fest, her mother can be heard in the background complaining about the length of time she has been on the phone. LeAnn ends the spot singing the company's jingle, "Simply connected, simply Samsung." LeAnn also did a print ad for the

National Fluid Milk Processor Promotion Board—best known for their Milk Mustache ads. In her ad, LeAnn admits that while she may sing about broken hearts, she will never sing about broken bones because she drinks tons of milk.

Not everything has resulted in gold records and starring TV roles for LeAnn. She has experienced some letdowns along the way. For example, even though her single of "How Do I Live" sold more than four million copies, it was rejected for the film *Con Air*—reportedly because LeAnn refused to change the song's arrangement and drop her father as producer. Trisha Yearwood got to record another version for the movie and went on to win a 1997 Grammy for Best Female Country Vocal.

Perhaps the biggest disappointment in LeAnn's fifteen years was her parents' 1997 divorce. She told the *Los Angeles Times*, "It was very traumatic. It was one of the hardest things I've ever been through. But things have gotten better. . . . I am very close to both of my parents. It's not one of those cases where families totally split up and never speak to each other again." In fact, as her manager, her father continues to travel with LeAnn, and her mother still heads her fan club back home.

Experiencing so much at such a young age—joy and heartache, successes and set-backs—LeAnn has had to grow up faster than most teens. People often comment that she is 15 going on 30. While most girls her age are going to school, playing sports, hanging out with their boyfriends, and being regular teenagers, LeAnn is all business. In fact, LeAnn takes pride in calling herself a business woman. She told *Seventeen* magazine, "The smartest thing I've ever done for myself is take control of what I do."

Because LeAnn has such a major hand in the business side of her career, she sometimes gets into disagreements about it with her parents. Says LeAnn, "My dad and I get into fights all the time about little things when we're on the road—and I usually end up winning. I think it comes down to: it's my life and if it's the right decision for me as a person, my parents understand that. I've had to learn to be independent at a young age and they've had to accept that early on. When it comes down to business, I think we separate that from our family relationship and we become business partners more than anything. We talk it out at that level, and then they go back to being parents."

LeAnn intends to remain deeply involved in all career decisions. "I know some artists aren't like this," she admits, "but I want to be involved in everything I do . . . all the money part, the business part. I've got albums, movies, TV stuff that people want me to do." LeAnn's nonstop career has left her little time for a personal life. Since she is never home, it is hard for her to meet people—especially boys. LeAnn confesses, "I'm very interested in guys, but I'm not going to find someone in a crowd. . . ."

These days, when she is not on stage performing, LeAnn can be found on the L.A.R. tour bus (her initials are painted on the side). The interior is fully fluffed out with soft

Busy as she is with tours and concerts, LeAnn finds time for charity events. She teamed up with Bryan White, another rising young country star, to perform a duet in their 1998 "Something to Talk About" concert to benefit the Special Olympics.

teal-green leather and a built-in 10-disc-changer stereo. LeAnn listens to everyone from Bonnie Raitt to Aerosmith to Prince. Her bus bedroom is just three-feet wide, six-feet long, and two-feet high. Jokes LeAnn, "You sleep with your feet forward, so you don't hit your head when the driver slams on the brakes."

No matter where her bus takes her, LeAnn manages to make time to study. Today, she takes classes through Texas Tech University. Her tutor, a friend of the family, rides the bus and helps LeAnn maintain her A average. Always a good student, LeAnn scored high enough on her Texas Tech entrance exams to skip the seventh and eighth grades.

But LeAnn is not all work. She also makes time to head to the mall and indulge in one of her favorite pastimes—shopping. She loves popping in at the Gap or at the local record stores to pick up new CDs from favorites like Alanis Morrisette or Vince Gill. Of course, she receives a lot of attention from other shoppers. But LeAnn takes everything in stride. "I have a Nike shirt that says I AM TIGER WOODS," she laughs. "And I love that shirt. I wear it everywhere I go. Because people come up and ask, 'Are you LeAnn Rimes?' And I say, 'No, can't you read my shirt? I'm Tiger Woods.'"

LeAnn's sense of humor and down-to-earth personality have helped make her one of the most popular country singers of all time, selling millions of records and earning millions of dollars. And she is just warming up. Besides scheduling more than 100 concert dates in 1998, she recorded a song, "Looking Through Your Eyes," for the Warner Brothers animated movie *Quest for Camelot* and also signed a three-picture deal with the studio. There is also talk of her starring in a movie next year and possibly a Broadway play beyond that.

As if her schedule was not already jam-packed, LeAnn also managed to find time to record her fourth album, appropriately titled *Sittin' on Top of the World*. The record is filled with a selection of songs that highlight LeAnn's diverse musical influences—from country to gospel to pop to rock. "The album is more of me, than anything," she says. "It shows the person that I am now, particularly the title.

LeAnn's joy in performing and her rapport with musicians and audiences are evident in her spirited performance at Long Island's Nassau Coliseum at the beginning of 1998. The young artist is steadfast in her determination "to make the best music I can and do the best concerts I can."

With all the good things that have happened to me, I have nothing to complain about."

At 16, LeAnn has accomplished things most adults can never hope to. She looks forward to the future and dreams of all the things she still wants to achieve. She would like to have her own house, high on a hill, with plenty of horses and cows. She would also like to help children and has plans to go to college and study speech pathology.

But real dreamers never stop dreaming. For LeAnn, there is always something new to strive for. "You know, you can mention Barbra Streisand to someone who listens to Aerosmith or Nine Inch Nails and they're going to know who she is," says LeAnn. "And that's my goal in life, to have everyone know, no matter what kind of music they listen to, who LeAnn Rimes is."

CHRONOLOGY

1982   Margaret LeAnn Rimes is born on August 28 in Flowood, Mississippi.

1988   Enters and wins her first talent contest; moves to Dallas, Texas; begins singing on the Dallas-Fort Worth Metroplex Opry circuit; auditions for the lead in *Annie II*.

1989   Begins performing in Johnnie High's Country Music Revue.

1990   Appears on *Star Search* and wins her category.

1993   Receives "Blue", a song originally written for Patsy Cline, from Bill Mark; records first independent label album *All That*; leaves school and begins study with a private tutor; Wilbur Rimes, LeAnn's father, quits his job to full-time manage LeAnn's career.

1994   *All That* released.

1995   Signs contract with Curb Records; records album *Blue*.

1996   *Blue* released and becomes number-one selling single for 20 weeks; films video *Blue*; first appearance at Fan Fair; first appearance at Grand Ole Opry; *Put a Little Holiday in Your Heart* released; becomes spokesperson for Target Stores; sings at White House Christmas Tree Lighting ceremony.

1997   Wins Song of the Year, Single Record of the Year, and Top New Female Vocalist from Academy of Country Music Awards; wins Best Female Country Vocal and Best New Artist from Grammy Awards; wins Horizon Award from the Country Music Association Awards; wins Female Star of Tomorrow from TNN-Music City News Country Awards; writes semi-autobiographical novel, *Holiday in Your Heart*; stars in *Holiday in Your Heart*, a made-for-TV movie; *Unchained Melody/ The Early Years* releases; *You Light Up My Life: Inspirational Songs* releases; becomes spokesperson for Samsung; takes classes through Texas Tech University; Belinda and Wilbur Rimes divorce.

1998   Signs a three-picture deal with Warner Brothers; records "Looking Through Your Eyes" for the Warner Brothers film *Quest for Camelot*; tours with Bryan White; *Sittin' On Top of the World* releases.

1999   Releases *LeAnn Rimes*; named one of *Teen People*'s hottest stars under 21.

2000   Releases single "I Love You" on the *Jesus* soundtrack.

Accomplishments

Discography

1994 *All That*

1996 *Blue*
   Put a Little Holiday in Your Heart

1997 *Unchained Melody/The Early Years*
   You Light Up My Life: Inspirational Songs

1998 *Sittin' on Top of the World*

1999 *LeAnn Rimes*

Video

1996 *Blue*

Book

1997 *Holiday in Your Heart*, with Tom Carter
   (semi-autobiographical novel)

Television

1997 *Holiday in Your Heart* (TV movie)
   Fan Fair Documentary (host)

1998 *Days of Our Lives* (guest star)

1999 *Moesha* (guest star)
   American Music Awards (host)

2000 *Class of 2000* (host)

Awards

1997 Song of the Year, Single Record of the Year, and Top New Female
   Vocalist from Academy of Country Music Awards; Best Female
   Country Vocal and Best New Artist from Grammy Awards; Horizon
   Award from the Country Music Association Awards; Female Star of
   Tomorrow from TNN-Music City News Country Awards.

Spokesperson

Target Stores

Samsung

National Fluid Milk Processor Promotion Board

FURTHER READING

Catalano, Grace. *Teen Country Queen*. New York: Bantam Doubleday Dell Books for Young Readers, 1997.

Hilburn, Robert. "Blue? Not This Girl." *Los Angeles Times*, March 26, 1998.

Hochman, David. "LeAnn Rimes." *Entertainment Weekly*, Year End Special, 1997.

Oliver, Lauren. "Get on the Bus with LeAnn Rimes." *Seventeen*, December 1997.

Rimes, LeAnn, and Tom Carter. *Holiday in Your Heart*. New York: Doubleday, 1997.

Sgammato, Jo. *Dream Come True: The LeAnn Rimes Story*. New York: Ballantine Books, 1997.

Switzer, Sara. "LeAnn Rimes." *Interview*, June 1998.

Websites
www.angelfire.com/co/leannworld

www.geocities.com/Nashville/5248

www.grandoleopry.com

www.leann-rimes.org

ABOUT THE AUTHOR

This is Cathy Alter Zymet's first book. Her articles have appeared in *Might*, *Spin*, and the *Washington City Paper*. She lives in Washington, D.C., with her husband and parakeet.

PHOTO CREDITS:
Reuters/Mike Segar/Archive Photos: 2; AP/Wide World Photos: 6, 9, 10, 12, 14, 26, 29, 32, 35, 38, 40, 46, 50, 57; Ron Wolfson/London Features Int'l, Ltd.: 17; Ron Wolfson/URW/London Features Int'l, Ltd.: 20; Ken Babolcsay/UBAB/London Features Int'l, Ltd.: 24; Reuters/John Kuntz/Archive Photos: 42; Reuters/Peter Morgan/Archive Photos: 45; London Features Int'l, Ltd.: 48; Ken Babolcsay/UBAB/London Features Int'l, Ltd.: 54; George De Sota/London Features Int'l, Ltd.: 59.

INDEX